Martin Luther King, Jr.

Champion of Civil Rights

Edith Hope Fine

Enslow Elementary

an imprint of

 Enslow Publishers, Inc.

40 Industrial Road   PO Box 38
Box 398   Aldershot
Berkeley Heights, NJ 07922   Hants GU12 6BP
USA   UK

http://www.enslow.com

To the Southern Poverty Law Center
and to all who honor Martin Luther King's dream
and work toward justice and fairness

Enslow Elementary, an imprint of Enslow Publishers, Inc.

Enslow Elementary® is a registered trademark of Enslow Publishers, Inc.

Library of Congress Cataloging-in-Publication Data

Fine, Edith Hope.
　　Martin Luther King, Jr. : champion of civil rights / Edith Hope Fine.
　　　　p. cm. — (Heroes of American history)
　　Includes index.
　　ISBN 0-7660-2466-0 (hardcover)
　　1. King, Martin Luther, Jr., 1929–1968—Juvenile literature. 2. African Americans—Biography—
Juvenile literature. 3. Civil rights workers—United States—Biography—Juvenile literature.
4. Baptists—United States—Clergy—Biography—Juvenile literature. 5. African Americans—Civil
rights—History—20th century—Juvenile literature.
　　I. Title. II. Series.
　　E185.97.K5F49　2006
　　323'.092—dc22　　　　　　　　　　　　　　　　　　2005009504

Printed in the United States of America

10 9 8 7 6 5 4 3 2 1

To Our Readers: We have done our best to make sure all Internet Addresses in this book were acti
and appropriate when we went to press. However, the author and the publisher have no control ov
and assume no liability for the material available on those Internet sites or on other Web sites they m
link to. Any comments or suggestions can be sent by e-mail to comments@enslow.com or to t
address on the back cover.

Every effort has been made to locate all copyright holders of material used in this book. If any erro
or omissions have occurred, corrections will be made in future editions of this book.

Illustration Credits: AP/Wide World, pp. 1, 3, 4, 6, 11, 14, 15, 18, 19, 21, 23, 24, 27, 28, 29
29B; Enslow Publishers, Inc., p. 25; Everett Collection, p. 8; From the Collections of Hen
Ford Museum & Greenfield Village, p. 13B; Library of Congress, pp. 9T, 20; Moorlan
Spingarn Research Center, Howard University, p. 17; Morehouse College, p. 9B; Nation
Archives, p. 12; Photographs and Prints Division, Schomburg Center for Research in Blac
Culture, The New York Public Library, Astor, Lenox and Tilden Foundations, pp. 7, 13T.

Cover Photographs: AP/Wide World (portrait); Library of Congress (background).

Table of Contents

Martin Luther King, Jr.

Chapter 1

"You Are As Good As Anyone"

Even when he was a young boy, Martin Luther King, Jr., dreamed of fairness for all people. He spent his life working to make that dream come true. Martin was born on January 15, 1929, in Atlanta, Georgia. His mother, Alberta, taught school. His father, Martin Luther Sr., was a minister. Martin grew up in a warm, loving family with his sister, Christine, and brother, Arthur Daniel (called A.D.).

Martin's nickname was M.L. He liked riding bikes and roller-skating. Quick to learn, he knew many church hymns and could recite long Bible verses from memory.

M.L.'s two best friends were both white. One day, they said he could not play with them anymore. Hurt, Martin asked why. His mother told him it had started long ago, when black people were slaves owned by white people. After slavery ended, white people still treated black people badly. Laws in the South kept blacks and whites apart.

No white children went to Martin's school. Signs on drinking fountains said WHITES ONLY. On buses, Martin

Martin was born in this house in Atlanta.

Martin, age six, at a birthday party
with other first graders.

and other African Americans had to sit in the back, apart from the white people, who sat in the better seats at the front of the bus.

Martin's father said to love all people, even when they were mean. His mother said, "You are as good as anyone else." Martin told his mother that someday he would turn the world "upside down."

From left: A.D., Christine, and Martin, with their parents and grandmother.

In high school, Martin played basketball, gave speeches, and read about African-American heroes like Frederick Douglass and Harriet Tubman. For him, school was easy. He skipped two grades and graduated when he was only fifteen.

Martin went to Morehouse College in Atlanta. There, he decided to become a minister. Two years later, he preached his first sermon at his father's church, stirring people with his big voice and big ideas.

Studying at a school in Pennsylvania, Martin learned about Mahatma Gandhi, a hero in the country of India. Gandhi had helped India become a free country no longer ruled by England.

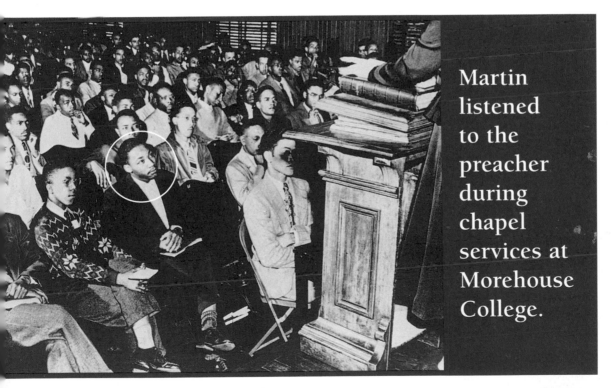

Gandhi taught his people that they did not have to fight to demand changes. He spoke out against violence. "All through history, the way of peace and love has won," he said.

Gandhi's ideas stayed with Martin. "I can't make myself believe that God wants me to hate," said Martin.

Martin admired Gandhi.

Martin listened to the preacher during chapel services at Morehouse College.

Chapter 2

"We Are Not Afraid"

Martin was studying religion at Boston University when he met a music student named Coretta Scott. Both Martin and Coretta loved books, music, and talking about ideas. They fell in love, and on June 18, 1953, they were married.

In 1954, the Supreme Court—the highest court in the United States—ruled that black students and white students could go to the same schools. This important law made Martin hopeful that the country was changing.

Martin finally finished all his schooling. Now he was called Dr. King and was the pastor of Dexter Avenue Baptist Church in Montgomery, Alabama.

In November 1955, Martin and Coretta welcomed their first baby girl, Yolanda. Three more children were born in the next few years: Dexter, Bernice, and Martin Luther III.

On December 2, 1955, a bus driver in Montgomery ordered Rosa Parks, a rider on his crowded bus, to stand up and give her seat to a white man. Rosa knew this was the

Martin and Coretta

The King family prays before eating.

law, but she also knew it was not right. She had worked all her life to help African Americans be treated better in the United States. She stayed in her seat until a policeman came and took her to jail.

The news of Rosa's arrest spread quickly. African

Americans were tired of unfair laws. They hated the law that made them sit at the back of the bus. What could they do? African-American leaders decided to start a bus boycott. They asked black people not to ride the city

Rosa Parks

buses the next Monday. If the buses stayed empty, the bus company would lose money. On Sunday, pastors preached about the boycott in their churches. No one knew what would happen. Thousands of African Americans usually rode the buses every day. They would have to find another way to get to work.

On Monday morning, Coretta looked out her window to see the buses drive down the street. They were almost empty. No black people were aboard.

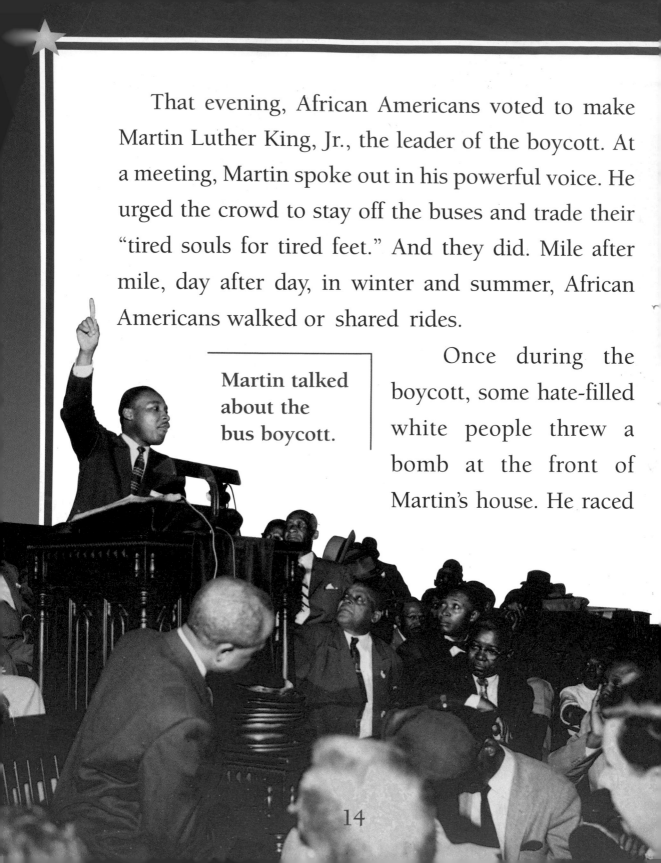

That evening, African Americans voted to make Martin Luther King, Jr., the leader of the boycott. At a meeting, Martin spoke out in his powerful voice. He urged the crowd to stay off the buses and trade their "tired souls for tired feet." And they did. Mile after mile, day after day, in winter and summer, African Americans walked or shared rides.

Martin talked about the bus boycott.

Once during the boycott, some hate-filled white people threw a bomb at the front of Martin's house. He raced

With the new law, Martin could at last sit near the front of this bus.

home, glad to find that his wife and baby were not hurt. Some angry blacks shouted that they would fight back, but Martin calmly asked them to "meet hate with love."

The Montgomery bus boycott lasted more than a year. Finally, the Supreme Court struck down the segregation laws that kept blacks and whites apart. From then on, all people—black or white—had a right to any seat on a city bus.

Martin's peaceful protest had worked.

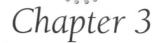

Chapter 3

"I Have a Dream Today"

In 1957, Martin became president of the SCLC,* a group started by the ministers of black churches to work against segregation. Martin was now known as an important civil rights leader. He traveled across the country to give many speeches about fairness for African Americans.

Martin went to Birmingham, Alabama, in 1963. There, blacks could not shop in the same stores or

* Southern Christian Leadership Conference

eat at the same restaurants as whites. The police chief, Eugene "Bull" Connor, hated African Americans, and he warned that he would not allow any protests in his city. "Let anybody just try to start something," he said, "and blood will run in the streets."

A group of people gathered to protest against segregation. They walked peacefully along the streets

Angry whites poured sugar and ketchup on the heads of protesters at this whites-only restaurant.

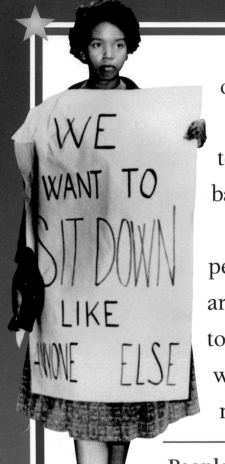

of Birmingham, saying that the city's laws were not fair to African Americans. True to Martin's ideas, they agreed not to fight back, even if force were used against them.

Bull Connor ordered the police to arrest people. Soon the jails were full. Martin was arrested, too. White ministers sent a letter to Martin in his jail cell. They said the city was not ready for change. They said it was not the right time to protest.

People carried signs to protest stores that were unfair to blacks.

Martin thought hard. Then he wrote a letter to the ministers with his answer: "For years now I have heard the word 'Wait!' . . . This 'wait' has almost always meant 'never.'" African Americans had been treated badly for hundreds of years. Martin believed the time had come for civil rights.

Soon students and children joined the peaceful march. Then something terrible happened. "Turn 'em back," ordered the police chief. The police attacked the young marchers with high-pressure fire hoses, dogs, and clubs. Across the United States, people were shocked by the violence they saw on the television news. "The eyes of the world are on Birmingham," said Martin.

Many people were badly hurt by the powerful force of the water.

That Sunday, another crowd began to march. Again, Bull Connor ordered the police to use hoses and dogs. But this time, his men did not obey.

Next, civil rights leaders came up with a big plan. They called for a march in the nation's capital to demand equal rights for all Americans.

On August 28, 1963, more than 250,000 people poured into Washington, D.C., from around the country. Old and young, white and black, rich and poor—all joined one of the biggest gatherings ever held in the United States.

People dotted every bit of space, crowding together in the center of the city. Millions more watched on television.

When Dr. King rose to speak, applause thundered in the hot summer air. Martin gazed out over the big crowd, then put down the paper with his written speech. Instead, he spoke from his heart.

"I have a dream," he began. Then he told them that he longed for a country where "my four little children will . . . not be judged by the color of their skin, but by the content of their character." He was saying that a person's ideas and feelings matter more than anything else.

Martin gave his most famous speech at the March on Washington.

The crowd sat still and hushed as Martin spoke. Many people wept.

Today, people still remember the important words Martin spoke that day.

Chapter 4

"I've Been to the Mountaintop"

I n 1964, Martin received the Nobel Peace Prize. It is the top honor in the world for a leader who works for peace. At thirty-five, Martin was the youngest person ever to win the prize. Soon after, a crowd in Atlanta—blacks and whites together—celebrated with Dr. King. "I've been to the mountaintop," he told them. " . . . But I must go back to the valley." It was his way of saying that there was still much more to be done.

In 1965 Martin went to Selma, Alabama. More than half the people in that city were African American, but few had been allowed to register to vote. The sheriff in Selma bragged that he would never treat black people as equal to whites.

Martin was proud to win the Nobel Peace Prize.

Martin put together a march to demand the right to vote. Once again, nonviolence was his tool, and protesters marched in the city. As Martin and many others were locked up in jail, more marchers took their places on the streets.

Then a teenage marcher was shot and killed. Martin knew he had to do something to protest the boy's death. When he was let out of jail, Martin planned a fifty-four-mile march from Selma to the state capital: Montgomery. Alabama's governor, George Wallace, ordered state police to stop the march.

Police attacked the marchers after they crossed this bridge.

As the marchers crossed a bridge in Selma, police charged into the peaceful crowd with tear gas, whips, and clubs. Seventy people were hurt and taken to the hospital. Reporters for newspapers and television spread news of the terrible violence in Selma. The reporters called this day "Bloody Sunday."

We Shall Overcome

Martin called for help. Many religious leaders from around the country traveled to Selma for another march. This time, as they reached the bridge, hundreds of white priests, ministers, and rabbis marched along with Martin. Many people, including whites and blacks, Christians and Jews, sang the hopeful words of the protest song "We Shall Overcome" during the five-day march.

"We Shall Overcome" became the most popular song of the civil rights movement.

President Lyndon Johnson had signed the Civil Rights Act in 1964. He signed the Voting Rights Act in 1965. These new laws gave equal rights to blacks and whites. Although change would not come quickly, the country was on a new path—a path of fairness for all Americans.

Chapter 5

"Free at Last"

Martin planned another march on Washington for April 1968 to help people of all races who were poor. It was called the Poor People's Campaign.

A few weeks before this march, African-American garbage workers in Memphis, Tennessee, went on strike. They were protesting low pay and unequal treatment by not going to work. Martin went to Memphis to show that he cared about the strikers.

"I may not get there with you," the thirty-nine-year-old preacher told a crowd on the night before the march. "But . . . we as a people will get to the promised land." Martin believed that someday, equal rights would win out.

The next morning, as Martin stepped outside his hotel room, a gunman shot him. Martin died instantly.

Word of Martin's death spread across a shocked country.

Martin is a hero of civil rights and of American history.

On the day of Martin's funeral, an old farm wagon pulled by two mules carried his casket. Nearly 100,000 people followed in silence.

On Martin's tombstone are words from his "I Have a Dream" speech: *Free at last. Free at last. Thank God Almighty, I'm free at last.*

Today, the name Martin Luther King, Jr., is known around the world. Each January, the United States honors him with a holiday—Martin Luther King, Jr., Day—to remember his leadership and courage.

All his life, Martin stayed true to his beliefs. He believed in peaceful action, and he inspired millions of Americans to work for justice and for change.

Martin Luther King, Jr., showed the power of one person to make a difference. His words and ideas still ring true, promising hope and calling people to action.

Timeline

1929~Born January 15 in Atlanta, Georgia.

1948~Becomes a Baptist minister.

1953~Marries Coretta Scott.

1954~Becomes pastor of Dexter Avenue Church in Montgomery, Alabama.

1955–56~Leads the bus boycott.

1963~Leads the March on Washington for Jobs and Freedom and gives "I Have a Dream" speech.

1964~Wins the Nobel Peace Prize.

1964–65~Leads civil rights marches in Alabama.

1968~Is shot and killed in Memphis, Tennessee.

1983~The U.S. Congress creates a national holiday to honor Martin.

1986~Martin Luther King, Jr., Day is celebrated for the first time around the country.

Words to Know

boycott—Refusing to buy a product or a service to protest something unfair.

civil rights movement—People working to gain equal rights under the law for all citizens.

nonviolence—Acting peacefully, without fighting.

protest—A public gathering to show disagreement and the need for change.

protest march—A nonviolent way for people to express their opinion.

segregation—Keeping different races apart in schools, restaurants, and other places.

slave—A person who is owned by another person and forced to work for no pay.

strike—Refusing to work as a way to protest unfair pay or working conditions.

Learn More

Books

Farris, Christine King. *My Brother Martin: A Sister Remembers Growing Up with the Rev. Dr. Martin Luther King Jr.* New York: Simon & Schuster Children's Publishing, 2003.

Pastan, Amy. *Martin Luther King, Jr.: A Photographic Story of a Life.* New York: DK Publishing, 2004.

Rappaport, Doreen. *Martin's Big Words: The Life of Dr. Martin Luther King, Jr.* New York: Hyperion Books for Children, 2001.

Internet Addresses

The King Center
  <http://www.thekingcenter.org/>

Quotes, photos, speeches, and more.
  <http://www.mlkonline.net/>

Index